HOP SCOTCH

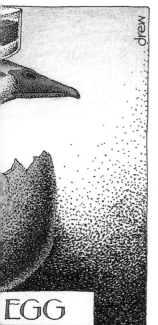

EGG

SCOTCH AND WATER

THE PLOT THICKENS

words
and drawings by
simon drew

sweet
f. a.

ACC EDITIONS

to caroline
and in memory of
joe bostock and ken drew
who both loved words

It is better to give
than to retrieve .

©2008 Simon Drew
World copyright reserved

ISBN 978-1-905377-29-9

British Library Cataloguing-in-Publication Data
A catalogue record for this book is available from the British Library

Printed in China
for the Antique Collectors' Club Ltd., Woodbridge, Suffolk

winnie the pie

WHO WILL SUCCEED
RICHARD III ?

has anyone got a hunch?

HAMLET

Prince of Denmork
in rotten state

ANT AND CLEO

ADULTERY ON THE NILE.
Does she give him
the needle ?

ROSENCRANTZ AND
GUILDENSTERN
are they really dead ?

'Othello'
dedicated to
JD and JD and JD
©simondrew.co.uk

VENICE MERCHANT

'WHERE'S MY POUND
OF FISH ?'
Is Shylock turning
vegetarian ? Is pound
of flesh kosher ?

4

Lawyers can be trusted
to do the things they ought.
But would it be guessed
the phrase they like best....

is "Settled out of court".

ponchos pilot

INN ON THE PORK

ED CHEF AND S

VINE WAITER

HENGEHOGS

simon drew

THE SEVEN STAGES

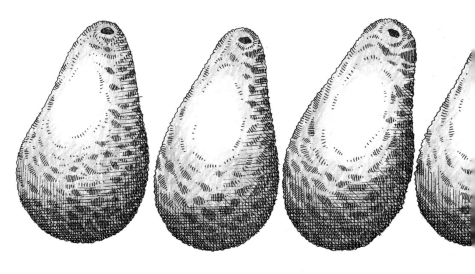

not
ripe

not
ripe

not
ripe

n
ri

12

OF THE AVOCADO

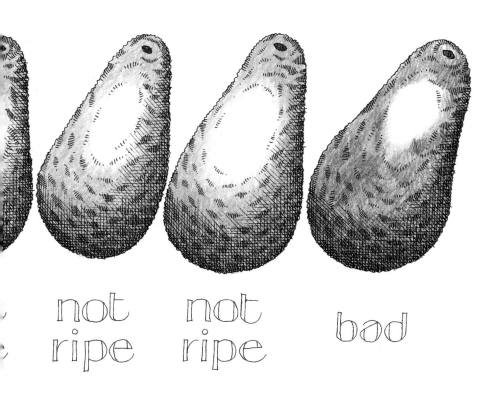

not
ripe

not
ripe

bad

one of the six waves of henry the VIII

simon drew

Housework is what a woman does that nobody notices unless she hasn't done it.

anon

CAT À
with a lit

simon drew

TONIC

e gin

17

Once more unto the beach
dear friends, once more.

simon drew

drew

drew

drew

23

a bit on the side

Mustard, ketchup, worcester sauce,
pickle, pepper, gravy, horse

radish, salad dressing, salt;
all washed down with single malt.

Resting under the north face of the aga

Drag the Magic Puffin

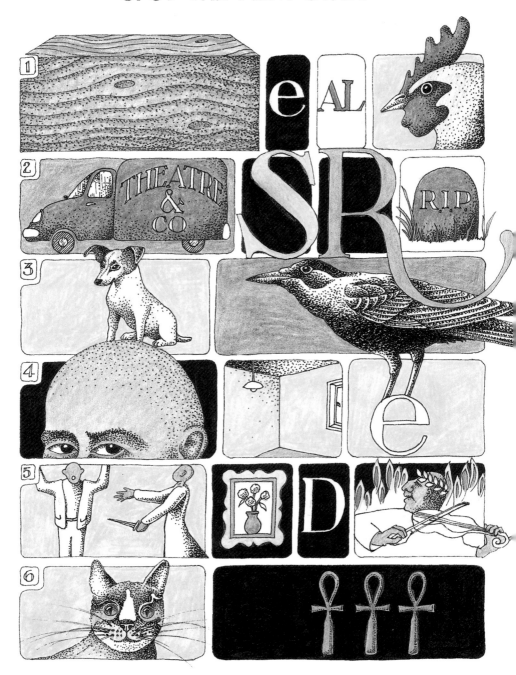

SPOT THE FILM STAR

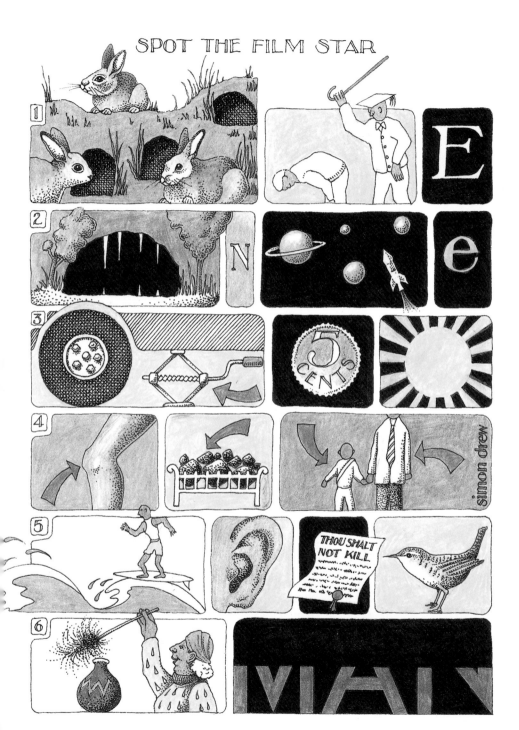

SPOT THE SHAKESPEARE CHARACTER

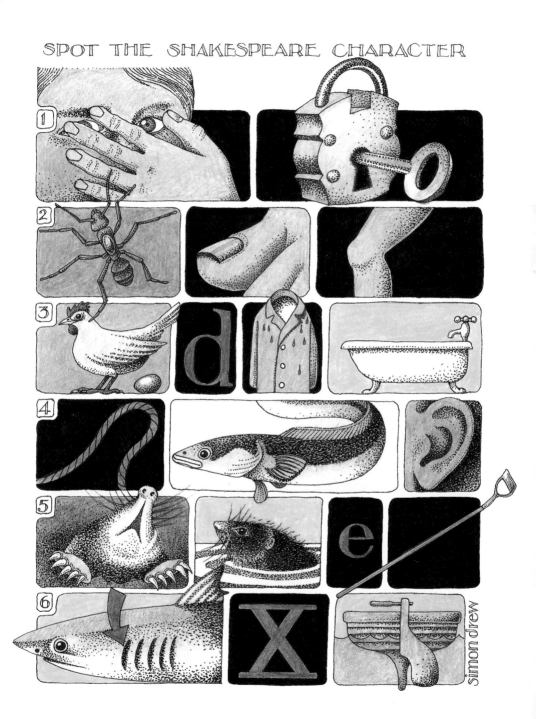

simon drew

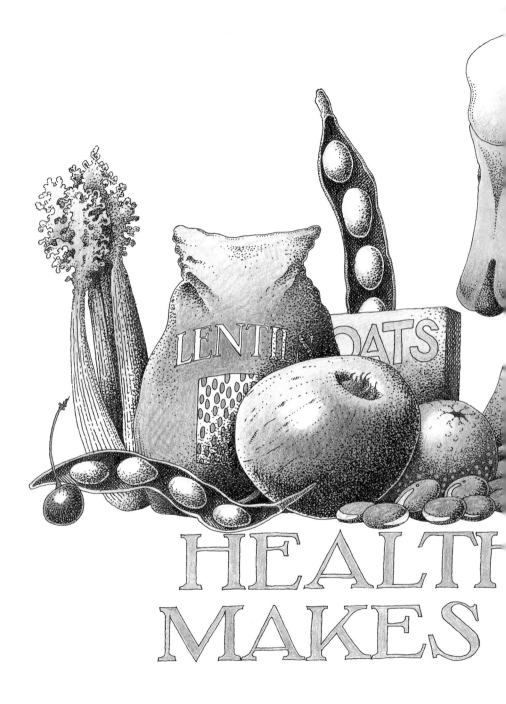

HEALTH

MAKES

FOOD
ME SICK

pre minstrel tension

emperor penguin,
king fish and
czar dean

36

a mystery explained

At the back of fashion stores,
changing clothes and tied in knots,
a leopard hides behind the doors
so no one sees it change its spots.

the lion, the witch
and the fitted bedroom furniture

three blonde mice
three blonde mice
see how they chat
see how they chat
they don't run after the farmer's wife
they're doing their nails with a carving knife
discussing the serious meaning of life
three blonde mice
three blonde mice

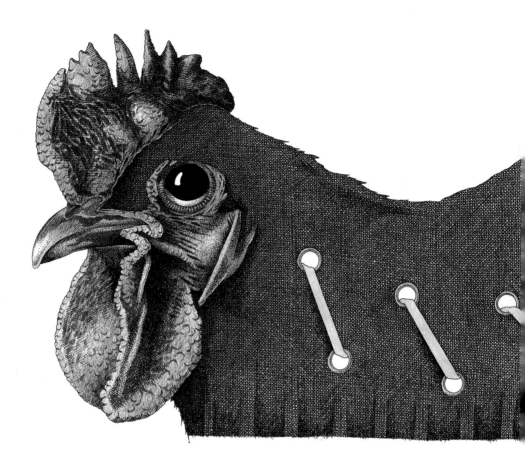

UNITED NOTIONS

The Beetle and The Reg were the very
best of friends.
Occasionally they'd fight and have to
make amends
so when they disagreed, a go-between
appeared,
always good at listening, often
slightly weird.

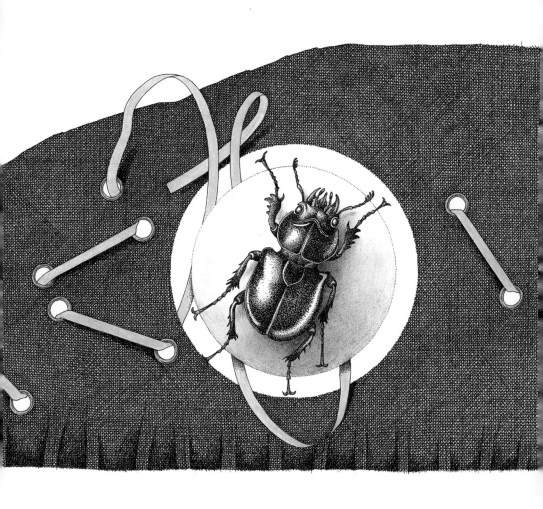

So all contentious issues were put
                    into a list:
eardrums hit with decibels,
                tables thumped with fist.
Somehow peace was settled as they
                reached their happy ends:
The Beetle and The Reg were the
                very best of friends.

41

PUT THE FOLLOWING IN CHRONOLOGICAL ORDER:

hell
freezing over

world
ending

plumber
arriving

wedding charms
explained

something old

something gnu

something burrowed

something blew

drew

suddenly
colin came to a fork in the road...

HEALTH IS WH
BEFORE WE

simon drew

46

T WE DRINK TO
FALL DOWN

When shall we three eat again?

simon drew

GOAT